KT-547-151

ESSENTIAL
Soups

p

Contents

Introduction

Soup was first made ten thousand years ago when the Egyptians prepared it by boiling ingredients in a large clay pot over an open fire and served it in shells or horns. Since then cooking methods and recipes have completely changed, but soup has continued to be an all-time favourite.

Indeed, the forerunner of all restaurants, the Baulangers Inn in Paris, had only soup on its menu. This is hardly surprising considering just how delicious soup is, especially today when the range of soups has become so wide. One of the most modern and appetising soups is made from Red (Bell) Peppers. This soup was even served, amongst other dishes, at the wedding reception of Victoria Adams (alias Posh Spice) and the Manchester United football star David Beckham when they requested a 'no-nonsense English meal'. In this book we add a tasty twist to this dish by including tomatoes in the recipe. Although you may not have the same invitation list as the happy couple, this soup and all the others in this book, will be sure to impress your guests.

Most soups are very nutritious, especially those which have a high vegetable content, while being inexpensive and also very filling. In fact, these are the reasons why it has been served in soup kitchens for many years. Surprisingly, it was Al Capone who founded this charity in Chicago in the 1930s. He actually paid $350 per day from his own finances to feed as many as 3000 unemployed people. However, it has been suggested that his actions were motivated not by human kindness but rather by the fact that he wanted to prevent people revealing the secrets of his criminal activities.

Soup is extremely easy to make, as it is simply a process of boiling a combination of meats, fish, or vegetables together. Certain consistencies are suitable for specific types of soup. For example, Gumbo tends to be thick, Chowder and Bouillabaisse are chunky, Consommé is thin and a Bisque is smooth. However, no strict rules apply when making soup as you can adjust any recipe to your preferred consistency.

Although soup is great served hot to warm you up in the winter, some soups can be served cold (such as Vichyssoise or many fruit soups) making them ideal for summer lunches or for light evening meals when served with a sandwich or salad. Garnishing with croûtons, grated cheese or soured cream often enhances the flavour of the soup while also improving its presentation.

Potato & Parsley Soup with Pesto

Serves 4

INGREDIENTS

3 slices rindless, smoked, fatty
  bacon
450 g/1 lb floury potatoes
450 g/1 lb onions
25 g/1 oz/2 tbsp butter
600 ml/1 pint/2^1/2 cups
  chicken stock
600 ml/1 pint/2^1/2 cups milk
100 g/3^1/2 oz/^{3}/4 cup
  dried conchigliette

150 ml/^{1}/4 pint/^{5}/8 cup double
  (heavy) cream
chopped fresh parsley
freshly grated Parmesan
  cheese and garlic bread, to
  serve

PESTO SAUCE:
60 g/2 oz/1 cup finely chopped
  fresh parsley

2 garlic cloves, crushed
60 g/2 oz/^{2}/3 cup pine nuts
  (kernels), crushed
2 tbsp chopped fresh basil
  leaves
60 g/2 oz/^{2}/3 cup freshly
  grated Parmesan cheese
white pepper
150 ml/^{1}/4 pint/^{5}/8 cup
  olive oil

1 To make the pesto sauce, process all of the ingredients in a blender or food processor for 2 minutes, or blend together by hand (see Cook's Tip).

2 Finely chop the bacon, potatoes and onions. Fry the bacon in a pan for 4 minutes. Stir in the butter, potatoes and onions and cook for 12 minutes.

3 Add the stock and milk to the pan, bring to the boil and simmer for 10 minutes. Add the pasta and simmer for a further 12-14 minutes.

4 Blend in the cream and simmer for 5 minutes. Add the parsley and 2 tbsp pesto sauce. Transfer the soup to serving bowls and serve with the Parmesan cheese and garlic bread.

COOK'S TIP

If you are making pesto by hand, it is best to use a mortar and pestle. Thoroughly grind together the parsley, garlic, pine nuts (kernels) and basil to make a smooth paste, then mix in the cheese and pepper. Finally, gradually beat in the oil.

Haricot (Navy) Bean & Pasta Soup

Serves 4

INGREDIENTS

250 g/9 oz/1^1/$_3$ cups haricot
(navy) beans, soaked for
3 hours in cold water and
drained
4 tbsp olive oil
2 large onions, sliced
3 garlic cloves, chopped
425 g/14 oz can chopped
tomatoes

1 tsp dried oregano
1 tsp tomato purée (paste)
850 ml/1^1/$_2$ pints/3^1/$_2$ cups
water
90 g/3^1/$_2$ oz/^{3}/$_4$ cup dried
fusilli or conchigliette
115 g/4 oz sun-dried
tomatoes, drained and
thinly sliced

1 tbsp chopped fresh
coriander (cilantro) or flat
leaf parsley
salt and pepper
2 tbsp Parmesan cheese
shavings, to serve

1 Put the haricot (navy)
beans in a large pan.
Cover with cold water and
bring to the boil. Boil
vigorously for 15 minutes.
Drain and keep warm.

2 Heat the oil in a pan
over a medium heat
and fry the onions for 2–3
minutes or until soft. Stir
in the garlic and cook for
1 minute. Stir in the
tomatoes, oregano and
tomato purée (paste).

3 Add the water and the
reserved beans to the
pan. Bring to the boil,
cover, then simmer for
about 45 minutes, or until
the beans are almost tender.

4 Add the pasta to the
pan and season to taste.
Stir in the sun-dried
tomatoes, bring back to the
boil, partly cover and
simmer for 10 minutes, or
until the pasta is tender, but
still firm to the bite.

5 Stir the herbs into the
soup. Ladle the soup
into warm serving bowls,
sprinkle with Parmesan
and serve.

COOK'S TIP

*If preferred, place the beans in
a pan of cold water and bring
to the boil. Remove from the
heat and leave the beans to
cook in the water. Drain
and rinse before using.*

Cream of Lemon & Chicken Soup with Spaghetti

Serves 4

INGREDIENTS

60 g/2 oz/4 tbsp butter
8 shallots, thinly sliced
2 carrots, thinly sliced
2 celery sticks (stalks), thinly sliced
225 g/8 oz boned chicken breasts, finely chopped

3 lemons
1.2 litres/2 pints/5 cups chicken stock
225 g/8 oz dried spaghetti, broken into small pieces
150 ml/1/4 pint/5/8 cup double (heavy) cream

salt and white pepper

TO GARNISH:
fresh parsley sprig
3 lemon slices, halved

1 Melt the butter in a large saucepan. Add the shallots, carrots, celery and chicken and cook over a low heat, stirring occasionally, for 8 minutes.

2 Thinly pare the lemons and blanch the lemon rind in boiling water for 3 minutes. Squeeze the juice from the lemons.

3 Add the lemon rind and juice to the pan,

together with the chicken stock. Bring slowly to the boil over a low heat and simmer for 40 minutes.

4 Add the spaghetti to the pan and cook for 15 minutes. Season with salt and white pepper and add the cream. Heat through, but do not allow the soup to boil.

5 Pour the soup into a tureen or individual

bowls, garnish with the parsley and half slices of lemon and serve immediately.

COOK'S TIP

You can prepare this soup up to the end of step 3 in advance, so that all you need do before serving is heat it through before adding the pasta and the finishing touches.

Chicken & Sweetcorn Soup

Serves 4

INGREDIENTS

450 g/1 lb boned chicken
breasts, cut into strips
1.2 litres/2 pints/5 cups
chicken stock

150 ml/^{1}/$_4$ pint/^{5}/$_8$ cup double
(heavy) cream
100 g/3^1/$_2$ oz/^{3}/$_4$ cup
dried vermicelli
1 tbsp cornflour (cornstarch)

3 tbsp milk
175 g/6 oz sweetcorn
(corn) kernels
salt and pepper

1 Put the chicken, stock and cream into a large saucepan and bring to the boil over a low heat. Reduce the heat slightly and simmer for about 20 minutes. Season with salt and pepper to taste.

2 Meanwhile, cook the vermicelli in lightly salted boiling water for 10-12 minutes, until just tender. Drain the pasta and keep warm.

3 Mix together the cornflour (cornstarch) and milk to make a smooth paste, then stir into the soup until thickened.

4 Add the sweetcorn (corn) and pasta to the pan and heat through.

5 Transfer the soup to a warm tureen or individual soup bowls and serve immediately.

COOK'S TIP

If you are short of time, buy ready-cooked chicken, remove any skin and cut it into slices.

VARIATION

For crab and sweetcorn soup, substitute 450 g/1 lb cooked crabmeat for the chicken breasts. Flake the crabmeat well before adding it to the saucepan and reduce the cooking time by 10 minutes. For a Chinese-style soup, substitute egg noodles for the vermicelli and use canned, creamed sweetcorn (corn).

Tuscan Veal Broth

Serves 4

INGREDIENTS

60 g/2 oz/^{1}/3 cup dried peas, soaked for 2 hours and drained
900 g/2 lb boned neck of veal, diced
1.2 litres/2 pints/5 cups beef or brown stock (see Cook's Tip)

600 ml/1 pint/2^1/2 cups water
60 g/2 oz/^{1}/3 cup barley, washed
1 large carrot, diced
1 small turnip (about 175 g/6 oz), diced
1 large leek, thinly sliced

1 red onion, finely chopped
100 g/3^1/2 oz chopped tomatoes
1 fresh basil sprig
100 g/3^1/2 oz/^{3}/4 cup dried vermicelli
salt and white pepper

1 Put the peas, veal, stock and water into a large saucepan and gently bring to the boil. Using a slotted spoon, skim off any scum that rises to the surface of the liquid.

2 When all of the scum has been removed, add the barley and a pinch of salt to the mixture. Simmer gently over a low heat for 25 minutes.

3 Add the carrot, turnip, leek, onion, tomatoes and basil to the pan, and season to taste. Simmer for about 2 hours, skimming the surface from time to time. Remove the pan from the heat and set aside for 2 hours.

4 Set the pan over a medium heat and bring to the boil. Add the vermicelli and cook for 12 minutes. Season with salt and pepper to taste and remove and discard the basil. Ladle into soup bowls and serve immediately.

COOK'S TIP

Brown stock is made with veal bones and shin of beef roasted with dripping (drippings) in the oven for 40 minutes. Transfer the bones to a pan, add sliced leeks, onion, celery and carrots, a bouquet garni, white wine vinegar and a thyme sprig and cover with water. Simmer over a very low heat for 3 hours. Strain and blot the fat from the surface with kitchen paper.

Hot & Sour Soup

Serves 4

INGREDIENTS

2 tbsp cornflour (cornstarch)
4 tbsp water
2 tbsp light soy sauce
3 tbsp rice wine vinegar
1/2 tsp ground black pepper
1 small fresh red chilli, finely chopped

1 egg
2 tbsp vegetable oil
1 onion, chopped
850 ml/1 1/2 pints/3 3/4 cups chicken or beef consommé
1 open-cap mushroom, sliced

50 g/1 3/4 oz skinless chicken breast, cut into very thin strips
1 tsp sesame oil

1 Blend the cornflour (cornstarch) with the water to form a smooth paste. Add the soy sauce, rice wine vinegar, pepper and chilli and mix together.

2 Break the egg into a separate bowl and beat well.

3 Heat the oil in a preheated wok and fry the onion for 1–2 minutes.

4 Stir in the consommé, mushroom and chicken and bring to the boil. Cook for 15 minutes or until the chicken is tender.

5 Pour the cornflour (cornstarch) mixture into the soup and cook, stirring, until it thickens.

6 As you are stirring, gradually drizzle the egg into the soup, to create threads of egg.

7 Sprinkle with the sesame oil and serve immediately.

COOK'S TIP

Make sure that the egg is poured in very slowly and that you stir continuously to create threads of egg and not large pieces.

Chinese Cabbage Soup

Serves 4

INGREDIENTS

450 g/1 lb pak choi
600 ml/1 pint/2$^{1}/_{2}$ cups
    vegetable stock
1 tbsp rice wine vinegar

1 tbsp light soy sauce
1 tbsp caster (superfine) sugar
1 tbsp dry sherry
1 fresh red chilli, thinly sliced

1 tbsp cornflour (cornstarch)
2 tbsp water

1 Trim the stems of the pak choi and shred the leaves.

2 Heat the stock in a large saucepan. Add the pak choi and cook for 10–15 minutes.

3 Mix the rice wine vinegar, soy sauce, sugar and sherry together. Add this mixture to the stock, together with the sliced chilli. Bring to the boil, lower the heat and cook for 2–3 minutes.

4 Blend the cornflour (cornstarch) with the water to form a smooth paste. Gradually stir the cornflour (cornstarch) mixture into the soup. Cook, stirring constantly, until it thickens. Cook for a further 4–5 minutes. Ladle the soup into individual warm serving bowls and serve immediately.

VARIATION

Boil about 2 tbsp rice in lightly salted water until tender. Drain and spoon into the base of the soup bowls. Ladle the soup over the rice and serve immediately.

COOK'S TIP

Pak choi, also known as bok choi or spoon cabbage, has long, white leaf stalks and fleshy, spoon-shaped, shiny green leaves. There are a number of varieties available, which differ mainly in size rather than flavour.

Tuscan Bean & Vegetable Soup

Serves 4

INGREDIENTS

1 medium onion, chopped
1 garlic clove, finely chopped
2 celery sticks, sliced
1 large carrot, diced
400 g/14 oz can chopped
   tomatoes
150 ml/5 fl oz/²/₃ cup Italian
   dry red wine

1.2 litres/2 pints/5 cups fresh
   vegetable stock
1 tsp dried oregano
425 g/15 oz can mixed beans
   and pulses
2 medium courgettes
   (zucchini), diced
1 tbsp tomato purée (paste)

salt and pepper

TO SERVE:
low-fat pesto sauce
crusty bread

1 Place the onion, garlic, celery and carrot in a large saucepan. Stir in the tomatoes, red wine, vegetable stock and oregano.

2 Bring the vegetable mixture to the boil, cover and leave to simmer for 15 minutes. Stir the beans and courgettes (zucchini) into the mixture, and continue to cook, uncovered, for a further 5 minutes.

3 Add the tomato purée (paste) to the mixture and season well with salt and pepper to taste. Then heat through, stirring occasionally, for 2–3 minutes, but do not allow the mixture to boil again.

4 Ladle the soup into warm bowls and top with a spoonful of low-fat pesto on each portion. Serve the soup accompanied with plenty of fresh crusty bread.

VARIATION

For a more substantial soup, add 350 g/12 oz diced lean cooked chicken or turkey with the tomato purée (paste) in step 3.

Creamy Sweetcorn Soup

Serves 4

1 large onion, chopped
1 large potato, peeled and
  diced
1 litre/1³/₄ pints/1 quart
  skimmed milk
1 bay leaf
¹/₂ tsp ground nutmeg

450 g/1 lb sweetcorn kernels,
  canned or frozen, drained
  or thawed
1 tbsp cornflour (cornstarch)
3 tbsp cold water
4 tbsp natural low-fat
  fromage frais
  (unsweetened yogurt)

salt and pepper

TO GARNISH:
100 g/3¹/₂ oz lean ham, diced
2 tbsp fresh chives, snipped

1 Place the onion and potato in a large pan and pour over the milk. Add the bay leaf, nutmeg and half the sweetcorn. Bring to the boil, cover and simmer for 15 minutes until the potato is softened. Stir occasionally and keep the heat low so that the milk does not burn on the bottom of the pan.

2 Discard the bay leaf and leave the liquid to cool for 10 minutes.

Transfer to a blender and process for a few seconds. Or, rub through a sieve.

3 Pour the smooth liquid into a pan. Blend the cornflour (cornstarch) with the water to make a paste and stir it into the soup.

4 Bring the soup back to the boil, stirring until it thickens, and add the remaining sweetcorn. Heat through for 2–3 minutes until piping hot.

5 Remove from the heat and season with salt and pepper to taste. Stir in the fromage frais (yogurt). Ladle the soup into warm bowls and serve sprinkled with the diced ham and snipped chives.

VARIATION

For a more substantial soup, add 225 g/8 oz flaked white crab meat or peeled prawns (shrimp) in step 4.

Chilled Piquant Prawn (Shrimp) & Cucumber Soup

Serves 4

INGREDIENTS

1 cucumber, peeled and diced
400 ml/14 fl oz/1²/³ cups
  fresh fish stock, chilled
150 ml/5 fl oz/²/³ cup tomato
  juice
150 ml/5 fl oz/²/³ cup low-fat
  natural (unsweetened)
  yogurt

150 ml/5 fl oz/²/³ cup low-fat
  fromage frais (or double
  the quantity of yogurt)
125 g/4¹/² oz peeled prawns
  (shrimp), thawed if frozen,
  roughly chopped
few drops Tabasco sauce
1 tbsp fresh mint, chopped

salt and white pepper
ice cubes, to serve

TO GARNISH:
sprigs of mint
cucumber slices
whole peeled prawns (shrimp)

1 Place the diced cucumber in a blender or food processor and work for a few seconds until smooth. Alternatively, chop the cucumber finely and push through a sieve.

2 Transfer the cucumber to a bowl. Stir in the stock, tomato juice, yogurt, fromage frais (if using) and prawns (shrimp), and mix well. Add the Tabasco

sauce and season with salt and pepper to taste.

3 Stir in the chopped mint, cover and chill for at least 2 hours.

4 Ladle the soup into glass bowls and add a few ice cubes. Serve garnished with sprigs of fresh mint, cucumber slices and whole peeled prawns (shrimp).

VARIATION

Instead of prawns (shrimp), add white crab meat or minced chicken. For a vegetarian version of this soup, omit the prawns (shrimp) and add an extra 125 g/4¹/² oz finely diced cucumber. Use fresh vegetable stock instead of fish stock.

Italian Cream of Tomato Soup

Serves 4

INGREDIENTS

60 g/2 oz/4 tbsp unsalted
butter
1 large onion, chopped
900 g/2 lb Italian plum
tomatoes, skinned and
roughly chopped

600 ml/1 pint/2^1/$_2$ cups
vegetable stock
pinch of bicarbonate of soda
(baking soda)
225 g/8 oz/2 cups dried fusilli
1 tbsp caster (superfine) sugar

150 ml/^{1}/$_4$ pint/^{5}/$_8$ cup double
(heavy) cream
salt and pepper
fresh basil leaves, to garnish
deep-fried croûtons, to serve

1 Melt the butter in a
pan and fry the onion
until softened. Add the
chopped tomatoes, with
300 ml/ ^{1}/$_2$ pint/1^1/$_4$ cups of
vegetable stock and the
bicarbonate of soda (baking
soda). Bring the soup to
the boil and simmer for
20 minutes.

2 Remove the pan from
the heat and set aside
to cool. Purée the soup in
a blender or food processor
and pour through a fine
strainer back into the
saucepan.

3 Add the remaining
vegetable stock and the
fusilli to the pan, and
season to taste.

4 Add the sugar to the
pan, bring to the boil,
then simmer for about
15 minutes.

5 Pour the soup into
warm soup bowls,
swirl the double (heavy)
cream around the surface
of the soup and garnish
with fresh basil leaves.
Serve immediately with
deep-fried croûtons.

VARIATION

*To make orange and tomato
soup, simply use half the
quantity of vegetable stock,
topped up with the same
amount of fresh orange juice
and garnish the soup with
orange rind. Or to make
tomato and carrot soup, add
half the quantity again of
vegetable stock with the
same amount of carrot juice
and 175 g/6 oz/1^1/$_4$ cups
grated carrot to the recipe,
cooking the carrot with
the onion.*

Lentil, Pasta & Vegetable Soup

Serves 4

INGREDIENTS

1 tbsp olive oil
1 medium onion, chopped
4 garlic cloves, finely chopped
350 g/12 oz carrot, sliced
1 stick celery, sliced
225 g/8 oz/1¹/4 cups red
   lentils

600 ml/1 pint/2¹/2 cups fresh
   vegetable stock
700 ml/1¹/4 pint/scant 3 cups
   boiling water
150 g/5¹/2 oz/scant 1 cup
   pasta

150 ml/5 fl oz/²/3 cup natural
   low-fat fromage frais
   (unsweetened yogurt)
salt and pepper
2 tbsp fresh parsley, chopped,
   to garnish

1 Heat the oil in a large saucepan and gently fry the prepared onion, garlic, carrot and celery, stirring gently, for 5 minutes until the vegetables begin to soften.

2 Add the lentils, stock and boiling water. Season with salt and pepper to taste, stir and bring back to the boil. Simmer, uncovered, for 15 minutes until the lentils are completely tender. Allow to cool for 10 minutes.

3 Meanwhile, bring another saucepan of water to the boil and cook the pasta according to the instructions on the packet. Drain well and set aside.

4 Place the soup in a blender and process until smooth. Return to a saucepan and add the pasta. Bring back to a simmer and heat for 2–3 minutes until piping hot. Remove from the heat and stir in the fromage frais (yogurt). Season if necessary.

5 Serve sprinkled with chopped parsley.

COOK'S TIP

Avoid boiling the soup once the fromage frais (yogurt) has been added. Otherwise it will separate and become watery, spoiling the appearance of the soup.

Tomato & Red (Bell) Pepper Soup

Serves 4

INGREDIENTS

2 large red (bell) peppers	600 ml/1 pint/2^1/$_2$ cups fresh	salt and pepper
1 large onion, chopped	vegetable stock	2 spring onions (scallions),
2 sticks celery, trimmed and	2 bay leaves	finely shredded, to garnish
chopped	2 x 400 g/14 oz cans plum	crusty bread, to serve
1 garlic clove, crushed	tomatoes	

1 Preheat the grill (broiler) to hot. Halve and deseed the (bell) peppers, arrange them on the grill (broiler) rack and cook, turning occasionally, for 8–10 minutes until softened and charred.

2 Leave to cool slightly, then carefully peel off the charred skin. Reserving a small piece for garnish, chop the (bell) pepper flesh and place in a large saucepan.

3 Mix in the onion, celery and garlic. Add the stock and the bay leaves. Bring to the boil, cover and simmer for 15 minutes. Remove from the heat.

4 Stir in the tomatoes and transfer to a blender. Process for a few seconds until smooth. Return to the saucepan.

5 Season to taste and heat for 3–4 minutes until piping hot. Ladle into warm bowls and garnish with the reserved (bell) pepper cut into strips and the spring onion (scallion). Serve with crusty bread.

COOK'S TIP

If you prefer a coarser, more robust soup, lightly mash the tomatoes with a wooden spoon and omit the blending process in step 4.

Carrot, Apple & Celery Soup

Serves 4

INGREDIENTS

900 g/2 lb carrots, finely diced
1 medium onion, chopped
3 sticks celery, diced
1 litre/1³/₄ pints/1 quart fresh
    vegetable stock

3 medium-sized eating
    (dessert) apples
2 tbsp tomato purée (paste)
1 bay leaf
2 tsp caster (superfine) sugar

¹/₄ large lemon
salt and pepper
celery leaves, washed and
    shredded, to garnish

1 Place the carrots, onion and celery in a large saucepan and add the stock. Bring to the boil, cover and simmer for 10 minutes.

2 Meanwhile, peel, core and dice 2 of the eating (dessert) apples. Add the pieces of apple, tomato purée (paste), bay leaf and caster (superfine) sugar to the saucepan and bring to the boil. Reduce the heat, half cover and allow to simmer for 20 minutes. Remove and discard the bay leaf.

3 Meanwhile, wash, core and cut the remaining apple into thin slices, leaving on the skin. Place the apple slices in a small saucepan and squeeze over the lemon juice. Heat gently and simmer for 1–2 minutes until tender. Drain and set aside.

4 Place the carrot and apple mixture in a blender or food processor and blend until smooth. Alternatively, press the carrot and apple mixture through a sieve with the back of a wooden spoon.

5 Gently re-heat the soup if necessary and season with salt and pepper to taste. Ladle the soup into warm bowls and serve topped with the reserved apple slices and shredded celery leaves.

COOK'S TIP

Soaking light coloured fruit in lemon juice helps to prevent it from turning brown.

Minestrone

Serves 8–10

INGREDIENTS

3 garlic cloves
3 large onions
2 celery sticks (stalks)
2 large carrots
2 large potatoes
100 g/3½ oz French (green)
  beans
100 g/3½ oz courgettes
  (zucchini)
60 g/2 oz/4 tbsp butter

50 ml/2 fl oz/¼ cup olive oil
60 g/2 oz rindless fatty bacon,
  finely diced
1.5 litres/2¾ pints/6⅞ cups
  vegetable or chicken stock
100 g/3½ oz chopped
  tomatoes
2 tbsp tomato purée (paste)
1 bunch fresh basil, finely
  chopped

100 g/3½ oz Parmesan
  cheese rind
85 g/3 oz dried spaghetti,
  broken up
salt and pepper
freshly grated Parmesan
  cheese, to serve

1 Finely chop the garlic, onions, celery, carrots, potatoes, beans and courgettes (zucchini).

2 Heat the butter and oil together in a large saucepan, add the bacon and cook for 2 minutes. Add the garlic and onion and fry for 2 minutes, then stir in the celery, carrots and potatoes and fry for a further 2 minutes.

3 Add the beans to the pan and fry for 2 minutes. Stir in the courgettes (zucchini) and fry for a further 2 minutes. Cover the pan and cook all the vegetables, stirring frequently, for 15 minutes.

4 Add the stock, tomatoes, tomato purée (paste), basil, and cheese rind and season to taste. Bring to the boil,

lower the heat and simmer for 1 hour. Remove and discard the cheese rind.

5 Add the spaghetti pieces to the pan and cook for 20 minutes. Serve in large, warm soup bowls sprinkled with freshly grated Parmesan cheese.

Ravioli alla Parmigiana

Serves 4

INGREDIENTS

285 g/10 oz Basic Pasta Dough
1.2 litres/2 pints/5 cups veal
   stock
freshly grated Parmesan
   cheese, to serve

FILLING:
100 g/3^1/2 oz/1 cup freshly
   grated Parmesan cheese
100 g/3^1/2 oz/1^2/3 cups fine
   white breadcrumbs
2 eggs

125 ml/4 fl oz/^{1}/2 cup
   Espagnole Sauce (see
   Cook's Tip, below)
1 small onion, finely chopped
1 tsp freshly grated nutmeg

1 Make the basic pasta dough. Carefully roll out 2 sheets of the pasta dough and cover with a damp tea towel (dish cloth) while you make the filling for the ravioli.

2 To make the filling, mix together the grated Parmesan cheese, white breadcrumbs, eggs, espagnole sauce (see Cook's Tip, right), chopped onion and the freshly grated nutmeg in a large mixing bowl.

3 Place spoonfuls of the filling at regular intervals on 1 sheet of pasta dough. Cover with the second sheet of pasta dough, then cut into squares and seal the edges.

4 Bring the veal stock to the boil in a large pan. Add the ravioli and cook for about 15 minutes.

5 Transfer the soup and ravioli to warm serving bowls and serve at once, generously sprinkled with Parmesan cheese.

COOK'S TIP

For espagnole sauce, melt 2 tbsp butter and stir in 25g/1 oz/^{1}/4 cup plain flour until smooth. Stir in 1 tsp tomato purée, 250 ml/ 9 fl oz/1^1/8 cups hot veal stock, 1 tbsp Madeira and 1^1/2 tsp white wine vinegar. Dice 25 g/1 oz each bacon, carrot and onion and 15 g/ ^{1}/2 oz each celery, leek and fennel. Fry with a thyme sprig and a bay leaf in oil. Drain, add to the sauce and simmer for 4 hours. Strain.

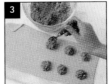

Pea & Egg Noodle Soup with Parmesan Cheese Croûtons

Serves 4

INGREDIENTS

3 slices smoked, rindless, fatty bacon, diced	2.3 litres/4 pints/10 cups chicken stock	chopped fresh parsley, to garnish
1 large onion, chopped	225 g/ 8 oz dried egg noodles	Parmesan cheese croûtons
15 g/$^1/_2$ oz/1 tbsp butter	150 ml/$^1/_4$ pint/$^5/_8$ cup double	(see Cook's Tip, below),
450 g/1 lb/2$^1/_2$ cups dried peas, soaked in cold water for 2 hours and drained	(heavy) cream salt and pepper	to serve

1 Put the bacon, onion and butter in a large pan and cook over a low heat for about 6 minutes.

2 Add the peas and the chicken stock to the pan and bring to the boil. Season lightly with salt and pepper, cover and simmer for 1½ hours.

3 Add the egg noodles to the pan and simmer for a further 15 minutes.

4 Pour in the cream and blend thoroughly. Transfer to soup bowls, garnish with parsley and top with Parmesan cheese croûtons (see Cook's Tip, right). Serve immediately.

VARIATION

Use other pulses, such as dried haricot (navy) beans, borlotti or pinto beans, instead of the peas.

COOK'S TIP

To make Parmesan cheese croûtons, cut a French stick into slices. Coat each slice lightly with olive oil and sprinkle with Parmesan cheese. Grill (broil) for about 30 seconds.

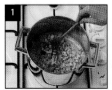

Smoked Haddock Soup

Serves 4–6

INGREDIENTS

8 oz smoked haddock fillet
1 onion, chopped finely
1 garlic clove, crushed
2 1/2 cups water

2 1/2 cups skimmed milk
1–1 1/2 cups hot mashed
  potatoes
2 tbsp butter
1 tbsp lemon juice

6 tbsp low-fat natural
  fromage frais
4 tbsp fresh parsley, chopped
salt and pepper

---

1 Put the fish, onion, garlic and water into a saucepan. Bring to a boil, cover, and simmer for 15–20 minutes.

2 Remove the fish from the pan, strip off the skin, and remove all the bones. Flake the flesh finely.

3 Return the skin and bones to the cooking liquid and simmer for 10 minutes. Strain, discarding the skin and bone. Pour the liquid into a clean pan.

4 Add the milk, flaked fish and seasoning to the pan, bring to a boil and simmer for about 3 minutes.

5 Gradually whisk in sufficient mashed potato to form a fairly thick soup, then stir in the butter, and adjust the taste with lemon juice.

6 Add the fromage frais and 3 tablespoons of the chopped parsley. Reheat gently and adjust the seasoning. Sprinkle with the remaining parsley and serve immediately.

COOK'S TIP

Undyed smoked haddock may be used in place of the bright yellow fish; it will give a paler colour but just as much flavour. Alternatively, use smoked cod or smoked white fish

Mussel & Potato Soup

Serves 4

INGREDIENTS

750 g/1 lb 10 oz mussels
2 tbsp olive oil
100 g/3^1/$_2$ oz/7 tbsp unsalted
  butter
2 slices rindless, fatty bacon,
  chopped
1 onion, chopped
2 garlic cloves, crushed

60 g/2 oz/^{1}/$_2$ cup plain
  (all purpose) flour
450 g/1 lb potatoes, thinly
  sliced
100 g/3^1/$_2$ oz/^{3}/$_4$ cup
  dried conchigliette
300 ml/^{1}/$_2$ pint/1^1/$_4$ cups
  double (heavy) cream

1 tbsp lemon juice
2 egg yolks
salt and pepper

TO GARNISH:
2 tbsp finely chopped fresh
  parsley
lemon wedges

1 Debeard the mussels and scrub them under cold water for 5 minutes. Discard any mussels that do not close immediately when sharply tapped.

2 Bring a large pan of water to the boil, add the mussels, oil and a little pepper and cook until the mussels open.

3 Drain the mussels, reserving the cooking liquid. Discard any mussels that are closed. Remove the mussels from their shells.

4 Melt the butter in a large saucepan and cook the bacon, onion and garlic for 4 minutes. Stir in the flour, then 1.2 litres/ 2 pints/5 cups of the reserved cooking liquid.

5 Add the potatoes to the pan and simmer for 5 minutes. Add the conchigliette and simmer for a further 10 minutes.

6 Add the cream and lemon juice, season to taste, then add the mussels to the pan.

7 Blend the egg yolks with 1-2 tbsp of the remaining cooking liquid, stir into the pan and cook for 4 minutes.

8 Ladle the soup into 4 warm individual soup bowls, garnish with the chopped fresh parsley and lemon wedges and serve.

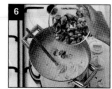

Chicken & Asparagus Soup

Serves 4

INGREDIENTS

225 g/8 oz fresh asparagus
850 ml/1$\frac{1}{2}$ pints/3$\frac{3}{4}$ cups
    fresh chicken stock
150 ml/5 fl oz/$\frac{2}{3}$ cup dry
    white wine

1 sprig each fresh parsley, dill
    and tarragon
1 garlic clove
60 g/2 oz/$\frac{1}{3}$ cup vermicelli
    rice noodles

350 g/12 oz lean cooked
    chicken, finely shredded
salt and white pepper
1 small leek

1 Wash the asparagus and trim away the woody ends. Cut each spear into pieces 4 cm/ 1½ inches long.

2 Pour the stock and wine into a large saucepan and bring to the boil.

3 Wash the herbs and tie them with clean string. Peel the garlic clove and add, with the herbs, to the saucepan together with the asparagus and noodles. Cover and simmer for 5 minutes.

4 Stir in the chicken and plenty of seasoning. Simmer gently for a further 3-4 minutes or until heated through.

5 Trim the leek, slice it down the centre and wash under running water to remove any dirt. Shake dry and shred finely.

6 Remove the herbs and garlic and discard.

7 Ladle the soup into warm bowls, sprinkle with shredded leek and serve at once.

VARIATION

You can use any of your favourite herbs in this recipe, but choose those with a subtle flavour so that they do not overpower the asparagus. Small, tender asparagus spears give the best results and flavour.

COOK'S TIP

Rice noodles contain no fat and are an ideal substitute for egg noodles.

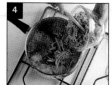

Clear Chicken & Egg Soup

Serves 4

INGREDIENTS

1 tsp salt
1 tbsp rice wine vinegar
4 eggs
850 ml/1¹/₂ pints/3³/₄ cups
   chicken stock

1 leek, sliced
125 g/4¹/₂ oz broccoli florets
125 g/4¹/₂ oz/1 cup shredded
   cooked chicken
2 open-cap mushrooms, sliced

1 tbsp dry sherry
dash of chilli sauce
chilli powder, to garnish

1 Bring a large saucepan of water to the boil and add the salt and rice wine vinegar. Reduce the heat so that it is just simmering and carefully break the eggs into the water, one at a time. Poach the eggs for 1 minute. Remove the poached eggs with a slotted spoon and set aside.

2 Bring the stock to the boil in a separate pan and add the leek, broccoli, chicken, mushrooms and sherry and season with chilli sauce to taste. Cook for 10–15 minutes.

3 Add the poached eggs to the soup and cook for a further 2 minutes. Carefully transfer the soup and poached eggs to 4 individual soup bowls. Dust with a little chilli powder to garnish and serve immediately.

COOK'S TIP

You could use 4 dried Chinese mushrooms, rehydrated according to the packet instructions, instead of the open-cap mushrooms, if you prefer.

VARIATION

You could substitute 125 g/4¹/₂ oz fresh or canned crabmeat or the same quantity of fresh or frozen cooked prawns (shrimp) for the chicken, if desired.

Curried Chicken & Sweetcorn (Corn) Soup

Serves 4

INGREDIENTS

175 g/6 oz can sweetcorn (corn), drained
850 ml/1½ pints/3¾ cups chicken stock
350 g/12 oz cooked, lean chicken, cut into strips

16 baby corn cobs
1 tsp Chinese curry powder
1-cm/½-inch piece fresh root ginger (ginger root), grated

3 tbsp light soy sauce
2 tbsp chopped chives

1 Place the canned sweetcorn (corn) in a food processor, together with 150 ml/¼ pint/⅔ cup of the chicken stock and process until the mixture forms a smooth purée.

2 Pass the sweetcorn purée through a fine sieve, pressing with the back of a spoon to remove any husks.

3 Pour the remaining chicken stock into a large pan and add the strips of cooked chicken. Stir in the sweetcorn (corn) purée.

4 Add the baby corn cobs and bring the soup to the boil. Boil the soup for 10 minutes.

5 Add the curry powder, ginger and soy sauce and cook for 10–15 minutes. Stir in the chives.

6 Transfer the soup to warm bowls and serve.

COOK'S TIP

Prepare the soup up to 24 hours in advance without adding the chicken, let cool, cover and store in the refrigerator. Add the chicken and heat the soup through thoroughly before serving.

Chick Pea (Garbanzo Bean) & Chicken Soup

Serves 4

INGREDIENTS

25 g/1 oz/2 tbsp butter
3 spring onions (scallions),
    chopped
2 garlic cloves, crushed
1 fresh marjoram sprig,
    finely chopped

350 g/12 oz boned chicken
    breasts, diced
1.2 litres/2 pints/5 cups
    chicken stock
350 g/12 oz can chick peas
    (garbanzo beans), drained
1 bouquet garni

1 red (bell) pepper, diced
1 green (bell) pepper, diced
115 g/4 oz/1 cup small dried
    pasta shapes, such as
    elbow macaroni
salt and white pepper
croûtons, to serve

1 Melt the butter in a large saucepan. Add the spring onions (scallions), garlic, sprig of fresh marjoram and the diced chicken and cook, stirring frequently, over a medium heat for 5 minutes.

2 Add the chicken stock, chick peas (garbanzo beans) and bouquet garni to the pan and season with salt and white pepper.

3 Bring the soup to the boil, lower the heat and then simmer gently for about 2 hours.

4 Add the diced (bell) peppers and pasta to the pan, then simmer for a further 20 minutes.

5 Transfer the soup to a warm tureen. To serve, ladle the soup into individual serving bowls and serve immediately, garnished with the croûtons.

COOK'S TIP

If preferred, use dried chick peas (garbanzo beans). Cover with cold water and set aside to soak for 5–8 hours. Drain and add the peas to the soup, according to the recipe, and allow an additional 30 minutes– 1 hour cooking time.

Carrot & Cumin Soup

Serves 4-6

INGREDIENTS

3 tbsp butter or margarine

1 large onion, chopped

1–2 garlic cloves, crushed

12 oz carrots, sliced

3 1/2 cups Chicken or Vegetable Stock

3/4 tsp ground cumin

2 celery sticks, sliced thinly

4 1/2 oz potato, diced

2 tsp tomato paste

2 tsp lemon juice

2 fresh or dried bay leaves

1 1/4 cups skimmed milk

salt and pepper

celery leaves, to garnish

1 Melt the butter or margarine in a large saucepan. Add the onion and garlic and fry very gently until the onion begins to soften.

2 Add the carrots and continue to fry gently for a further 5 minutes, stirring frequently and taking care they do not brown.

3 Add the stock, cumin, seasoning, celery, potato, tomato paste, lemon juice and bay leaves and bring to a boil. Cover and simmer gently for about 30 minutes until all the vegetables are very tender.

4 Discard the bay leaves, cool the soup a little, and then press it through a strainer or blend in a food processor or blender until smooth.

5 Pour the soup into a clean pan, add the milk and bring slowly to a boil. Taste and adjust the seasoning.

6 Garnish each serving with a small celery leaf and serve.

COOK'S TIP

This soup can be frozen for up to 3 months. Add the milk when reheating.

Italian Fish Soup

Serves 4

60 g/2 oz/4 tbsp butter
450 g/1 lb assorted fish fillets, such as red mullet and snapper
450 g/1 lb prepared seafood, such as squid and prawns (shrimp)
225 g/8 oz fresh crabmeat
1 large onion, sliced

25 g/1 oz/$^1/_4$ cup plain (all purpose) flour
1.2 litres/2 pints/5 cups fish stock
100 g/3$^1/_2$ oz/$^3/_4$ cup dried pasta shapes, such as ditalini or elbow macaroni
1 tbsp anchovy essence

grated rind and juice of 1 orange
50 ml/2 fl oz/$^1/_2$ cup dry sherry
300 ml/$^1/_2$ pint/1$^1/_4$ cups double (heavy) cream
salt and black pepper
crusty brown bread, to serve

1 Melt the butter in a large saucepan and cook the fish fillets, seafood, crabmeat and onion over a low heat for 6 minutes.

2 Stir the flour into the mixture.

3 Gradually add the fish stock and bring to the boil, stirring constantly. Reduce the heat and simmer for 30 minutes.

4 Add the pasta and cook for 10 minutes.

5 Stir in the anchovy essence, orange rind, orange juice, sherry and double (heavy) cream. Season to taste.

6 Heat the soup until completely warmed through. Transfer the soup to a tureen or to warm soup bowls and serve with crusty brown bread.

COOK'S TIP

The heads, tails, trimmings and bones of most non-oily fish can be used to make fish stock. Simmer 900 g/2 lb fish pieces in a pan with 150 ml/5 fl oz white wine, 1 chopped onion, 1 sliced carrot, 1 sliced celery stick (stalk), 4 black peppercorns, 1 bouquet garni and 1.75 litres/3 pints/7$^1/_2$ cups water for 30 minutes, then strain.

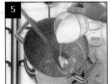

Mediterranean-style Fish Soup

Serves 4

INGREDIENTS

1 tbsp olive oil
1 large onion, chopped
2 garlic cloves, finely chopped
425 ml/15 fl oz/1³/4 cups
    fresh fish stock
150 ml/5 fl oz/²/3 cup dry
    white wine
1 bay leaf
1 sprig each fresh thyme,
    rosemary and oregano

450 g/1 lb firm white fish
    fillets (such as cod,
    monkfish or halibut),
    skinned and cut into
    2.5 cm/1 inch cubes
450 g/1 lb fresh mussels,
    prepared
400 g/14 oz can chopped
    tomatoes

225 g/8 oz peeled prawns
    (shrimp), thawed if frozen
salt and pepper
sprigs of thyme, to garnish

TO SERVE:
lemon wedges
4 slices toasted French bread,
    rubbed with cut garlic
    clove

1 Heat the oil in a large pan and gently fry the onion and garlic for 2–3 minutes until just softened.

2 Pour in the stock and wine and bring to the boil. Tie the bay leaf and herbs together with clean string and add to the saucepan together with the fish and mussels. Stir well, cover and simmer for 5 minutes.

3 Stir in the tomatoes and prawns (shrimp) and continue to cook for a further 3–4 minutes until piping hot and the fish is cooked through.

4 Discard the herbs and any mussels that have not opened. Season and ladle into warm bowls. Garnish with sprigs of thyme and serve with lemon wedges and toasted bread.

COOK'S TIP

Traditionally, the toasted bread is placed at the bottom of the bowl and the soup spooned over the top. For convenience, look out for prepared, cooked shellfish mixtures, which you could use instead of fresh fish. Simply add to the soup with the tomatoes in step 3.

Fish Soup with Wontons

Serves 4

INGREDIENTS

125 g/4¹/₂ oz large, cooked,
   peeled prawns (shrimp)
1 tsp chopped chives
1 small garlic clove, finely
   chopped
1 tbsp vegetable oil

12 wonton wrappers
1 small egg, beaten
850 ml/1¹/₂ pints/3³/₄ cups
   fish stock
175 g/6 oz white fish fillet,
   diced

dash of chilli sauce
sliced fresh red chilli and
   chives, to garnish

1 Roughly chop a quarter of the prawns (shrimp) and mix together with the chopped chives and garlic.

2 Heat the oil in a preheated wok and stir-fry the prawn (shrimp) mixture for 1–2 minutes. Remove from the heat and set aside to cool completely.

3 Spread out the wonton wrappers on a work surface (counter). Spoon a little of the prawn (shrimp) filling into the centre of each wonton wrapper. Brush the edges of the wonton wrappers with beaten egg and press the edges together, scrunching them to form a 'moneybag' shape. Set aside while you are preparing the soup.

4 Pour the fish stock into a large saucepan and bring to the boil. Add the diced white fish and the remaining prawns (shrimp) and cook for 5 minutes.

5 Season to taste with the chilli sauce. Add the wontons and cook for a further 5 minutes. Spoon into warmed serving bowls, garnish with sliced red chilli and chives and serve immediately.

VARIATION

Replace the prawns (shrimp) with cooked crabmeat for an alternative flavour.

Crab & Ginger Soup

Serves 4

INGREDIENTS

1 carrot, chopped
1 leek, chopped
1 bay leaf
850 ml/1^1/$_2$ pints/3^3/$_4$ cups
    fish stock

2 medium-sized cooked crabs
2.5-cm/1-inch piece fresh root
    ginger (ginger root), grated
1 tsp light soy sauce

^{1}/$_2$ tsp ground star anise
salt and pepper

1 Put the carrot, leek, bay leaf and stock into a large pan and bring to the boil. Reduce the heat, cover and simmer for 10 minutes, or until the vegetables are nearly tender.

2 Meanwhile, remove all of the meat from the cooked crabs. Break off the claws, break the joints and remove the meat (you may require a fork or skewer for this). Add the crabmeat to the saucepan of fish stock.

3 Add the ginger, soy sauce and star anise to the fish stock and bring to the boil. Leave to simmer for about 10 minutes, or until the vegetables are tender and the crab is heated through. Season.

4 Ladle the soup into warmed serving bowls and garnish with crab claws. Serve at once.

COOK'S TIP

If fresh crabmeat is unavailable, use drained canned crabmeat or thawed frozen crabmeat instead.

COOK'S TIP

To prepare cooked crab, loosen the meat from the shell by banging the back of the underside with a clenched fist. Stand the crab on its edge with the shell towards you. Force the shell from the body with your thumbs. Twist off the legs and claws and remove the meat. Twist off the tail; discard. Remove and discard the gills. Cut the body in half along the centre and remove the meat. Scoop the brown meat from the shell with a spoon.

Shrimp Dumpling Soup

Serves 4

INGREDIENTS

DUMPLINGS:
150 g/5^1/2 oz/1^5/8 cups plain
   (all-purpose) flour
50 ml/2 fl oz/^{1}/4 cup boiling
   water
25 ml/1 fl oz/^{1}/8 cup cold
   water
1^1/2 tsp vegetable oil

FILLING:
125 g/4^1/2 oz minced (ground)
   pork
125 g/4^1/2 oz cooked peeled
   shrimp, chopped
50 g/1^3/4 oz canned water
   chestnuts, drained, rinsed
   and chopped
1 celery stick, chopped
1 tsp cornflour (cornstarch)

1 tbsp sesame oil
1 tbsp light soy sauce

SOUP:
850 ml/1^1/2 pints/3^3/4 cups
   fish stock
50 g/1^3/4 oz cellophane
   noodles
1 tbsp dry sherry
chopped chives, to garnish

---

1 To make the
dumplings, mix the
flour, boiling water, cold
water and oil in a bowl until
a pliable dough is formed.

2 Knead the dough on a
floured surface for
5 minutes. Cut the dough
into 16 equal-sized pieces.

3 Roll the dough pieces
into rounds 7.5 cm/
3 inches in diameter.

4 Mix the filling
ingredients together.

5 Spoon a little of the
filling mixture into the
centre of each round. Bring
the edges of the dough
together, scrunching them
up to form a 'moneybag'
shape. Twist to seal.

6 Pour the fish stock into
a large saucepan and
bring to the boil.

7 Add the cellophane
noodles, dumplings
and dry sherry to the pan
and cook for 4–5 minutes,
until the noodles and
dumplings are tender.
Garnish and serve.

COOK'S TIP

*Wonton wrappers may be
used instead of the dumpling
dough if time is short.*

Beef, Water Chestnut & Rice Soup

Serves 4

INGREDIENTS

350 g/12 oz lean beef (such as
  rump or sirloin)
1 litre/1³/4 pints/1 quart fresh
  beef stock
1 cinnamon stick, broken
2 star anise
2 tbsp dark soy sauce

2 tbsp dry sherry
3 tbsp tomato purée (paste)
115 g/4 oz can water
  chestnuts, drained and
  sliced
175 g/6 oz/3 cups cooked
  white rice

1 tsp zested orange rind
6 tbsp orange juice
salt and pepper

TO GARNISH:
strips of orange rind
2 tbsp chives, snipped

1 Carefully trim away any fat from the beef. Cut the beef into thin strips and then place into a large saucepan.

2 Pour over the stock and add the cinnamon, star anise, soy sauce, sherry, tomato purée (paste) and water chestnuts. Bring to the boil, skimming away any surface scum with a flat ladle. Cover the pan and simmer gently for about 20 minutes or until the beef is tender.

3 Skim the soup with a flat ladle to remove any scum again. Remove and discard the cinnamon and star anise. Blot the surface with absorbent kitchen paper to remove any fat.

4 Stir in the rice, orange rind and juice. Season with salt and pepper to taste. Heat through for 2–3 minutes before ladling into warm bowls. Serve the soup garnished with strips of orange rind and snipped chives.

VARIATION

Omit the rice for a lighter soup that is an ideal starter for an Oriental meal of many courses. For a more substantial soup that would be a meal in its own right, add diced vegetables such as carrot, (bell) pepper, sweetcorn or courgette (zucchini).

Winter Beef & Vegetable Soup

Serves 4

INGREDIENTS

60 g/2 oz/^{1}/₃ cup pearl barley
1.2 litres/2 pints/5 cups fresh
  beef stock
1 tsp dried mixed herbs

225 g/8 oz lean rump or
  sirloin beef
1 large carrot, diced
1 leek, shredded
1 medium onion, chopped

2 sticks celery, sliced
salt and pepper
2 tbsp fresh parsley, chopped,
  to garnish
crusty bread, to serve

1 Place the pearl barley in a large saucepan. Pour over the stock and add the mixed herbs. Bring to the boil, cover and simmer for 10 minutes.

2 Trim any fat from the beef and cut the meat into thin strips.

3 Skim away any scum that has risen to the top of the stock.

4 Add the beef, carrot, leek, onion and celery to the pan. Bring back to the boil, cover and simmer for about 20 minutes or until the meat and vegetables are just tender.

5 Skim away any remaining scum that has risen to the top of the soup with a flat ladle. Blot the surface with absorbent kitchen paper to remove any fat. Season with salt and pepper to taste.

6 Ladle the soup into warm bowls and sprinkle with freshly chopped parsley. Serve accompanied with plenty of crusty bread.

VARIATION

This soup is just as delicious made with lean lamb or pork fillet. A vegetarian version can be made by omitting the beef and beef stock and using vegetable stock instead. Just before serving, stir in 175 g/ 6 oz fresh bean curd (tofu), drained and diced. An even more substantial soup can be made by adding other root vegetables, such as swede or turnip, instead of, or as well as, the carrot.

Peking Duck Soup

Serves 4

INGREDIENTS

125 g/4½ oz lean duck breast
    meat
225 g/8 oz Chinese leaves
    (cabbage)

850 ml/1½ pints/3¾ cups
    chicken or duck stock
1 tbsp dry sherry or rice wine
1 tbsp light soy sauce
2 garlic cloves, crushed

pinch of ground star anise
1 tbsp sesame seeds
1 tsp sesame oil
1 tbsp chopped fresh parsley

1 Remove the skin from the duck breast and finely dice the flesh.

2 Using a sharp knife, shred the Chinese leaves (cabbage).

3 Put the stock in a large saucepan and bring to the boil.

4 Add the sherry or rice wine, soy sauce, diced duck meat and shredded Chinese leaves and stir to mix thoroughly. Reduce the heat and leave to simmer for 15 minutes.

5 Stir in the garlic and star anise and cook over a low heat for 10–15 minutes, or until the duck is tender.

6 Dry-fry the sesame seeds in a preheated, heavy-based frying pan (skillet) or wok, stirring.

7 Remove the sesame seeds from the pan and stir them into the soup, together with the sesame oil and parsley.

8 Spoon the soup into warm bowls and serve.

COOK'S TIP

If Chinese leaves (cabbage) are unavailable, use leafy green cabbage instead. You may wish to adjust the quantity to taste, as Western cabbage has a stronger flavour and odour than Chinese leaves (cabbage).

Beef & Vegetable Noodle Soup

Serves 4

INGREDIENTS

225 g/8 oz lean beef
1 garlic clove, crushed
2 spring onions (scallions), chopped
3 tbsp soy sauce

1 tsp sesame oil
225 g/8 oz egg noodles
850 ml/1$^1/_2$ pints/3$^3/_4$ cups beef stock
3 baby corn cobs, sliced

$^1/_2$ leek, shredded
125 g/4$^1/_2$ oz broccoli, cut into florets (flowerets)
pinch of chilli powder

1 Using a sharp knife, cut the beef into thin strips and place them in a shallow glass bowl.

2 Add the garlic, spring onions (scallions), soy sauce and sesame oil and mix together well, turning the beef to coat. Cover and leave to marinate in the refrigerator for 30 minutes.

3 Cook the noodles in a saucepan of boiling water for 3–4 minutes. Drain the noodles thoroughly and set aside until required.

4 Put the beef stock in a large saucepan and bring to the boil.

5 Add the beef, together with the marinade, the baby corn, leek and broccoli. Cover and leave to simmer over a low heat for 7–10 minutes, or until the beef and vegetables are tender and cooked through.

6 Stir in the noodles and chilli powder and cook for a further 2–3 minutes. Transfer to bowls and serve immediately.

COOK'S TIP

Vary the vegetables used, or use those to hand. If preferred, use a few drops of chilli sauce instead of chilli powder, but remember it is very hot!

Lamb & Rice Soup

Serves 4

INGREDIENTS

150 g/5¹/2 oz lean lamb
50 g/1³/4 oz/¹/4 cup rice
850 ml/1¹/2 pints/3³/4 cups
    lamb stock

1 leek, sliced
1 garlic clove, thinly sliced
2 tsp light soy sauce
1 tsp rice wine vinegar

1 medium open-cap
    mushroom, thinly sliced
salt

1 Using a sharp knife, trim any fat from the lamb and cut the meat into thin strips. Set aside until required.

2 Bring a large pan of lightly salted water to the boil and add the rice. Bring back to the boil, stir once, reduce the heat and cook for 10–15 minutes, until tender. Drain, rinse under cold running water, drain again and set aside until required.

3 Meanwhile, put the lamb stock in a large saucepan and bring to the boil.

4 Add the lamb strips, leek, garlic, soy sauce and rice wine vinegar to the stock in the pan. Reduce the heat, cover and leave to simmer for 10 minutes, or until the lamb is tender and cooked through.

5 Add the mushroom slices and the rice to the pan and cook for a further 2–3 minutes, or until the mushroom is completely cooked through.

6 Ladle the soup into 4 individual warmed soup bowls and serve immediately.

COOK'S TIP

Use a few dried Chinese mushrooms, rehydrated according to the packet instructions and chopped, as an alternative to the open-cap mushroom. Add the Chinese mushrooms with the lamb in step 4.

Veal & Ham Soup with Sherry

Serves 4

INGREDIENTS

60 g/2 oz/4 tbsp butter
1 onion, diced
1 carrot, diced
1 celery stick (stalk), diced
450 g/1 lb very thinly sliced
    veal
450 g/1 lb thinly sliced ham

60 g/2 oz/$^1/_2$ cup plain
    (all purpose) flour
1 litre/1$^3/_4$ pints/4$^3/_8$ cups
    beef stock
1 bay leaf
8 black peppercorns
pinch of salt

3 tbsp redcurrant jelly
150 ml/$^1/_4$ pint/$^5/_8$ cup cream
    sherry
100 g/3$^1/_2$ oz/$^3/_4$ cup dried
    vermicelli
garlic croûtons, to serve

1 Melt the butter in a large saucepan. Cook the onions, carrot, celery, veal and ham over a low heat for 6 minutes.

2 Sprinkle over the flour and cook, stirring, for a further 2 minutes. Gradually stir in the stock, then add the bay leaf, peppercorns and salt. Bring to the boil and simmer for 1 hour.

3 Remove from the heat and add the redcurrant jelly and cream sherry. Set aside for about 4 hours.

4 Discard the bay leaf from the pan and reheat the soup over a low heat until warmed through.

5 Meanwhile, cook the vermicelli in a pan of lightly salted boiling water for 10-12 minutes. Stir the vermicelli into the soup and transfer to warm soup bowls. Serve with garlic croûtons (see Cook's Tip, right).

COOK'S TIP

To make garlic croûtons, remove the crusts from 3 slices of day-old white bread. Cut the bread into 5 mm/$^1/_4$ inch cubes. Heat 3 tbsp olive oil over a low heat and stir-fry 1–2 finely chopped garlic cloves for 1–2 minutes. Remove the garlic and add the bread. Cook, stirring frequently, until golden brown. Remove from the pan and drain on kitchen paper (towels).

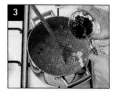

Veal & Wild Mushroom Soup with Vermicelli

Serves 4

INGREDIENTS

450 g/1 lb veal, thinly sliced
450 g/1 lb veal bones
1.2 litres/2 pints/5 cups water
1 small onion
6 peppercorns
1 tsp cloves

pinch of mace
140 g/5 oz oyster and shiitake
 mushrooms, roughly
 chopped
150 ml/^{1}/4 pint/^{5}/8 cup double
 (heavy) cream

100 g/3^1/2 oz/^{3}/4 cup dried
 vermicelli
1 tbsp cornflour (cornstarch)
3 tbsp milk
salt and pepper

1 Put the veal, bones and water into a large saucepan. Bring to the boil and lower the heat. Add the onion, peppercorns, cloves and mace and simmer for about 3 hours, until the veal stock is reduced by one-third.

2 Strain the stock, skim off any fat on the surface with a slotted spoon, and pour the stock into a clean saucepan. Add the veal meat to the pan.

3 Add the mushrooms and cream, bring to the boil over a low heat and simmer for 12 minutes. Meanwhile, cook the vermicelli in lightly salted boiling water until tender, but still firm to the bite. Drain and keep warm.

4 Mix together the cornflour (cornstarch) and milk to form a smooth paste. Stir into the soup to thicken. Season to taste with salt and pepper and just before serving, add the vermicelli. Transfer the soup to a warm tureen and serve immediately.

COOK'S TIP

You can make this soup with the more inexpensive cuts of veal, such as breast or neck slices. These are lean and the long cooking time ensures that the meat is really tender.

Mulligatawny Soup

Serves 4

INGREDIENTS

3 tbsp butter or margarine

1 large onion, chopped

2 carrots, chopped

2–3 celery sticks, chopped

1 dessert apple, peeled, cored
and chopped

1 tbsp all-purpose flour

1–2 tsp Madras curry powder

1–2 tsp curry paste

1/2 tsp ground coriander

5 cups Beef, Chicken or
Vegetable Stock

8 oz can chopped tomatoes

1/2 cup cooked long grain rice
(optional)

1/3–1/2 cup cooked chicken, beef
or lamb, chopped very finely

salt and pepper

poppadoms, to serve (optional)

---

1 Melt the butter or
margarine in a large
saucepan and fry the onion,
carrots, celery and apple,
stirring occasionally, until
just soft and lightly browned.

2 Stir in the flour, curry
powder, curry paste
and coriander and cook for
1 minute or so, stirring all
the time.

3 Gradually add the
stock and bring to a
boil, stirring constantly.

4 Add the tomatoes and
plenty of seasoning, cover
the pan, and simmer for about
45 minutes until the vegetables
and apple are tender.

5 Cool the soup a little,
then press through a
strainer or blend in a food
processor or blender until
smooth. Pour the soup into
a clean pan.

6 Add the rice (if using)
and the chicken or
meat, adjust the seasoning,

and bring to a boil.
Simmer gently for
5 minutes.

7 Serve the soup in
warmed bowls, with
poppadoms (if using).

This is a Parragon Book
First published in 1999
Parragon
Queen Street House
4 Queen Street
Bath BA1 1HE, UK

ISBN: 0-75253-354-1

Printed in China

Note
Cup measurements in this book are for American cups. Tablespoons are assumed to be 15 ml.
Unless otherwise stated, milk is assumed to be full fat, eggs are medium and pepper is
freshly ground black pepper.